MEDIEVAL ARTILLERY

Books LLC®, Wiki Series, Memphis, USA, 2011. ISBN: 9781156894705. www.booksllc.net
Copyright: http://creativecommons.org/licenses/by-sa/3.0/deed.en

Table of Contents

Abus gun	1
Bombard (weapon)	1
Early thermal weapons	2
Greek fire	10
Gunpowder artillery in the Middle Ages	14
Mons Meg	18
Ribauldequin	20
Trebuchet	20

Introduction

Purchase of this book entitles you to a free trial membership in the publisher's book club at www.booksllc.net. (Time limited offer.) Simply enter the barcode number from the back cover onto the membership form. The book club entitles you to select from hundreds of thousands of books at no additional charge. You can also download a digital copy of this and related books to read on the go. Simply enter the title or subject onto the search form to find them.

Each chapter in this book ends with a URL to a hyperlinked online version. Type the URL exactly as it appears. If you change the URL's capitalization it won't work. Use the online version to access related pages, websites, footnotes, tables, color photos, updates. Click the version history tab to see the chapter's contributors. Click the edit link to suggest changes.

A large and diverse editor base collaboratively wrote the book, not a single author. After a long process of discussion and debate, the chapters gradually took on a neutral point of view reached through consensus. Additional editors expanded and contributed to chapters striving to achieve balance and comprehensive coverage. This reduced the regional or cultural bias found in many other books and provided access and breadth on subject matter otherwise little documented.

Abus gun

The **Abus gun** is an early form of howitzer or more likely a bazooka created by the Ottoman empire. They were small, but often too heavy to carry, and many were equipped with a type of tripod. They had a caliber between 3 and 9 inches (230 mm) and fired a projectile weighing 4.25 pounds. Abus guns, despite being a form of howitzer, were primarily used as an anti-infantry weapon.

Military history

Background

Its origins are not known. Early artillery such as this gun opened the way for the developments in artillery that we have made across the ages, and spawned more recent and familiar types of artillery. They continued to develop it; by the Napoleonic era,

Each regiment of foot artillery was made up of 10 cannons; four of the older, heavy Balyemez and Sahi cannons, two of the older, lighter Abus guns and four of the new French-designed field guns... each of which came in a bewildering range of sizes. The *Balyemez* were massive, long-range guns...*Sahi* was the Ottoman word for "field," and therefore Sahi artillery meant simply field artillery... The Abus guns were a form of howitzer and came in 10- and 7centimeter diameter bores. The French-design guns were known as SuratTopcusu (speed artillery) because of their greater mobility."

Mechanics

Abus guns were a short-barreled artillery machine that fired shots about the size of a human fist. They also had many varieties of artillery, from large siege Bombard to the mobile Abus guns in question. Though light enough to carry, they needed to be equipped with a tripod of sorts. This movability was opposed to locating them in a guarded artillery emplacement, where versatility of the weapon would have been considerably restricted. The design remained unchanged until 1830 when the Prussian military advisers appointed by the sultan made a few minor improvements, standardising the weapons in order to improve efficiency.

Source http://en.wikipedia.org/wiki/Abus_gun

Bombard (weapon)

A **bombard** is a large-caliber, muzzle-loading medieval cannon or mortar, used chiefly in sieges for throwing heavy stone balls. The name **bombarde** was first noted and sketched in a French historical text around 1380. The modern term *bombardment* derives from this.

Bombards were usually used during sieges to hurl various forms of missile into enemy fortifications. Projectiles such as stone or metal balls, burning materials and weighted cloth soaked in quicklime or Greek fire are documented.

The name derives from medieval Latin and French forms from a Greek word expressing the making of a humming noise.

Notable examples

A notable example of a bombard is the large Mons Meg weapon, built around 1449 and used by King James II of Scotland. It was very powerful and used for bringing down castle walls. Mons Meg was capable of firing 180 kg (396 lb) shots and was one of the largest bombards in its time. It is now housed on public display at Edinburgh Castle. Other known 15th century superguns include the wrought-iron Pumhart von Steyr and Dulle Griet as well as the cast-bronze Faule Mette, Faule Grete, and Grose Bochse. The Tsar Cannon is a late 16th century show-piece.

The Dardanelles Gun, built in the Ottoman Empire in 1464 by Munir Ali, with a weight of 18.6 t and a length of 518 cm, was capable of firing stone balls of up to 63 cm diameter.

Eventually bombards were superseded by weapons using smaller calibre iron projectiles with more powerful gunpowder.

Gallery

"Hand bombard", 1390–1400

200kg wrought iron bombard, circa 1450, Metz, France. It was manufactured by forging together iron bars, held in place by iron rings. It fired 6kg stone balls. Length: 82cm.

The Dardanelles Gun.

Source http://en.wikipedia.org/wiki/Bombard_(weapon)

Early thermal weapons

The Siege and Destruction of Jerusalem by the Romans Under the Command of Titus, A.D. 70, by David Roberts (1850), shows the city burning

Early thermal weapons were devices or substances used in warfare during the classical and medieval periods (approx 8th century BC until the mid-16th century AD) which used heat or burning action to destroy or damage enemy personnel, fortifications or territories.

Incendiary devices were frequently used as projectiles during warfare, particularly during sieges and naval battles; some substances were boiled or heated to inflict damage by scalding or burning. Other substances relied on their chemical properties to inflict burns or damage. These weapons or devices could be used by individuals, manipulated by war machines, or utilised as army strategy.

The simplest, and most common, thermal projectiles were boiling water and hot sand, which could be poured over attacking personnel. Other antipersonnel weapons included the use of hot pitch, oil, resin, animal fat and other similar compounds. Smoke was used to confuse or drive off attackers. Substances such as quicklime and sulfur could be toxic and blinding.

Fire and incendiary weapons were used against enemy structures and territory, as well as personnel, sometimes on a massive scale. Large tracts of land, towns and villages were frequently destroyed as part of a scorched earth strategy. Incendiary mixtures, such as the oil-based Greek fire, could be launched by throwing machines or administered through a siphon. Sulfur- and oil-soaked materials were sometimes ignited and thrown at the enemy, or attached to spears, arrows and bolts and fired by hand or machine. Some siege techniques—such as mining and boring—relied on combustibles and fire to complete the collapse of walls and structures.

Towards the latter part of the period, gunpowder was invented, which increased the sophistication of the weapons, and led to the eventual development of the cannon and other firearms. Development of the early weapons has continued ever since, with a number of modern war weapons, such as napalm, flame throwers, and other explosives having direct roots in the original early thermal weapons. Fire-raising and other destructive strategies can still be seen in modern strategic bombing.

> " Behold from your walls the lands laid waste with fire and sword, booty driven off, the houses set on fire in every direction and smoking. "
> —Livy, The History of Rome

The destruction of enemy possessions and territory was a fundamental strategy of war, serving the dual purpose of punishment and deprivation of resources. Until the 5th century BC, the Greeks had little expertise in siege warfare and relied on a strategy of devastation to draw the enemy out; they destroyed crops, trees and houses. Centuries later, the Byzantines recommended this strategy, even though they had developed siege technology.

Fire was the easiest way of harrying and destroying territories, and could be done easily and quickly by small forces. It was a strategy put to good use by the Scots during the Wars of Independence; they repeatedly launched raids into northern England, burning much of the countryside until the whole region was transformed. King Edward II of England pursued one raiding party in 1327 by following the lights of burning villages.

" War without fire is like sausages without mustard "
—Jean Juvénal des Ursins on Henry V's firing of Meaux in 1421

The tactics were replicated by England during the Hundred Years' War; fire became their chief weapon as they laid waste to the French countryside during lightning raids called chevauchées, in a form of economic warfare. One estimate records the destruction of over 2000 villages and castles during one raid in 1339.

As well as causing the destruction of lands, foods and belongings, fire could also be used to divert manpower. 13th century Mongol armies regularly sent out small detachments from their main forces to start grass fires and fire settlements as diversions.

Devastation by fire was not only used as an offensive tactic; some countries and armies employed 'scorched earth' policies on their own land to deprive invading armies of all food and forage. Robert I of Scotland reacted to the English invasion of 1322 by launching punitive and diversionary chevauchées into north-west England, then retreating to Culross, burning as he went the Scottish lands which lay in the path of the English army. The English ran out of food and had to abandon the campaign. Kitchener employed scorched earth tactics to subdue Boer forces in South Africa when three years of warfare had resulted in a stalemate.

Such acts of aggression were not limited to wars against territorial enemies, but could form part of the strategies of conquest, subjugation and punishment of rebellion. Alexander the Great suppressed a revolt in Thebes, Greece in 335 BC, after which he ordered the city to be torched and laid waste. Alexander ordered (or allowed) a similar arson at Persepolis in 330 BC. It was a policy which was repeated throughout the period. Following his conquest of England in the 11th century, William I of England asserted his control of Northumbria by destructive campaigns throughout the region: "He ordered that crops and herds, tools and food should be burned to ashes. More than 100,000 people perished of hunger", reported Orderic Vitalis, a contemporary chronicler. It was a scene repeated the following century, during the anarchy of Stephen of England's reign. Civil war erupted between Stephen's supporters and those of the Empress Matilda, a rival claimant for the throne. The *Gesta Stephani* tells of the deeds of one of Stephen's supporters, Philip of Gloucester, by describing how he "raged in all directions with fire and sword, violence and plunder", reducing territory to "bare fields and dreadful desert".

Techniques of use

Normans use torches to fire the wooden keep on a motte at Dinan, 1064, Bayeux Tapestry

At the simplest level, fire itself was used as a weapon to cause large-scale destruction, or to target specific enemy positions or machinery. It was frequently used against siege engines and wooden structures. Incendiary weapons could be used to set fire to towns and fortifications, and a wide range of thermal weapons were used against enemy personnel. Some armies developed specialised "fire-troops". By 837, many Muslim armies had groups of "naffatin" (fire archers), and when the Mamluk Sultanate raised a fleet for an attack on Cyprus they had "nafata", or firetroops.

Simple fire-raising

The burning of enemy positions and equipment was not necessarily a complicated procedure, and many fires were set by individuals using common materials. When William I of England's army besieged Mayenne in 1063, they shot fire into the castle to panic the garrison, while two boys stole into the castle in order to start a fire within. The garrison surrendered.

Besieged forces would sometimes launch sorties in an attempt to fire the attackers camps or equipment. When Hugh Capet besieged Laon in 986–987, his troops became drunk one night, and Duke Charles's men sallied forth and torched the camp, forcing Hugh to abandon the siege.

The besieged were not the only ones who might fire siege equipment; when Frederick I Barbarossa abandoned his siege of Alessandria in 1175, he burned his own camp and equipment.

However, like all weapons, fire-raising had its own dangers. In 651 Penda of Mercia attempted to win Bamburgh Castle by building a pyre at its base from planks, beams, wattle and thatch. The wind changed direction and the fire blew back on Penda's men, who had to abandon the attack. This fortuitous wind-change was credited to Saint Aidan, who saw the smoke from the Farne Islands and prayed for the defenders.

Throwing machines

A number of throwing machines were in use throughout the classical and medieval periods. Generally referred to as "artillery", these engines could hurl, fire or shoot missiles and most could be used or adapted for throwing thermal weapons, by attacking and defending forces. Barrels, fire pots and other breakable containers of pitch, Greek fire, and other incendiary mixtures

1869 engraving showing a 13th century trebuchet launching an incendiary missile

could be thrown; other machines fired arrows and bolts, which could be ignited, or adapted to carry flammable mixtures. From the 12th century, Muslims in Syria were using clay and glass grenades for fire weapons, thrown by machines.

Most of the terms used for throwing machines were vague, and could refer to a number of specific engines, and all went through a number of changes and developments over the period. Among the most common were the ballista, mangonel and trebuchet. The ballista was similar in form to a crossbow, though much larger, and used a string-winding mechanism to fire a missile or bolt placed in a groove. Other giant crossbows were used throughout the period, and an "espringal", based on the ballista, which threw large bolts, was developed in the 13th century. Torsion-powered arrow firers had been used from 400 BC, and were adapted for stones. A mangonel had a wooden spoon-shaped arm, to hold a stone or object, which was manipulated under tension from a twisted rope. The trebuchet was an advanced development of the 12th or 13th century, which used a counter-weight to power the throwing arm, and was the major siege engine until the cannon became widespread.

In mining

Forces attacking a castle of other strong fortification sometimes sought to undermine the foundations by digging "mines" or tunnels underneath them. Usually, such mining or digging machinery was protected by a *tortoise* (also called a *cat*, *sow*, or *owl*): a covered shed on wheels, which protected the miners from missile attack.

As the tunnels were constructed, they were generally supported by wooden beams and posts. Once the mine had been finished, the internal space was filled with combustibles, such as brushwood, firewood, resin, and other incendiary substances; once ignited, these would burn the supporting props, causing the mine to collapse, bringing down with it the structures lying above. From the 15th century, gunpowder was also used, although the aim remained to burn the props.

Defenders might sometimes dig counter-tunnels in order to reach the enemy's mines and launch an attack; frequently thermal weapons were used to drive the besiegers from the tunnels.

Rather than undermining a structure, some besiegers used borers to drill holes in the outer walls in an effort to destroy them; such methods were more effective than rams on brick walls (which tended to absorb the shocks from the ram). Borers differed in size and mechanism, but a typical machine was made from a log of wood, tipped with iron and supported and driven by windlasses or ropes. Once a series of holes had been bored along the length of a wall, the holes were typically filled with rods of dry wood, saturated with sulfur or pitch and then ignited. Bellows could be used to encourage a blaze.

Fire ships

Fire ships were used on a number of occasions throughout the period. In 332 BC Alexander the Great laid siege to Tyre, a coastal base of the Phoenicians. In order to bring his siege engines within range, Alexander ordered the construction of moles. The Tyrians responded by attacking the first mole with a large fireship, which destroyed it. A large horse transport ship was packed with cedar torches, pitch, dried brush and other combustibles; above this were suspended cauldrons of sulfur, bitumen and "every sort of material apt to kindle and nourish flame". This was towed to the mole, and lit by the Phoenicians before they jumped overboard and swam

Chinese fire ships from the Wujing Zongyao military manuscript, 1044, Song Dynasty.

away.

Another example occurred during the 886 Siege of Paris, when the Vikings filled three warships with combustible material and pulled them upriver in a failed attempt to destroy the Franks' fortified bridges. Fire ships containing straw and powder were also used during the Chinese Battle of Lake Poyang in 1363.

Other methods

Often ingenious methods were developed for administering the weapons. The 10th-century Olga of Kiev is reported to have tied burning tinder to birds which, when released, flew back to their nests in the hostile town and set them alight. Siege towers and ladders could be fitted with a long, narrow tilting beam at the top, gouged with a groove, so that hot oil and water could be poured down on the enemy defenders during an escalade.

During an attack, castle or fortification defenders could launch or pour the substances on the heads of attackers below. This could be done over the battlements, but also through purpose-built holes such as machicolations and murder-holes. Indian records suggest smoke and fire was used defensively within a fortress to confuse and disorientate attackers; iron grills could also be heated and used to block passageways. During night attacks, defenders could drop lighted bundles over the walls so the enemy could be seen; Chinese and Muslim sources also describe the light gained by torches hung on the walls.

Use against stone castles

Stone castles were susceptible to fire, since they contained many combustible materials. In 1139, Henry de Tracy forced the surrender of Torrington Castle by the simple expedient of tossing lighted torches through the keep's loopholes.

Stone was also susceptible to intense heat, which would cause it to crack and collapse. Byzantine sources recorded the demolition of stone structures caused by placing clay pots of burning charcoal at the base of walls moistened with vinegar or urine, and the 6th century treatise by an engineer in Justinian's army includes the lighting fires beneath the walls amongst its instructions for sieges.

Stone castles sometimes offered other inflammatory targets. During the Crusades, Muslim defenders frequently hung bundles of straw against their walls as buffers against stones and rams; in turn, the Crusader archers would set these alight with fire arrows.

Defence against thermal attack

Defence from thermal weapons and fire attacks was usually water or other liquids such as urine; hides were soaked and draped over vulnerable wooden hoardings and siege engines, and vats and barrels of liquid were collected and stored by defenders and attackers. Hides were hung in an overlapping manner so that any water would run down the whole structure to extinguish flames. Some thermal weapons (such as quicklime or oil) could not be extinguished or eased by water, in which case sand or earth could be used. Wooden structures were frequently soaked in alum to increase their fire resistance. The Romans covered their *tortoises* (mobile siege sheds) with raw hides packed with vinegar-soaked seaweed or chaff, to serve as protection against regular and incendiary missiles. Throughout the period, sacks or nets might be filled with vinegar-moistened chaff, seaweed or wet moss and hung on the exterior. The wooden siege engines of the Crusaders were vulnerable to attack from the Byzantine and Muslim fire-weapons, so the troops inside siege towers kept stores of water and vinegar.

During the High Middle Ages, the majority of Poland's castles were still made of wood, so uncut stone was frequently added to the front to improve their fire defences.

Both attackers and defenders needed to be prepared for incendiary and thermal attack. When the Athenians besieged Syracuse in 416 BC they lost many siege engines to fire. The Syracusan ruler Dionysius I must have taken note of his success, for when he laid siege to Motya in 398 BC he organised special fire "brigades", who successfully doused the fires when his siege engines were bombarded.

Types of weapons

Flaming arrows, bolts, spears and rockets

Lit torches (burning sticks) were likely the earliest form of incendiary device. They were followed by incendiary arrows, which were used throughout the ancient and medieval periods. The simplest flaming arrows had oil- or resin-soaked tows tied just below the arrowhead and were effective against wooden structures. Both the Assyrians and the Judeans used fire arrows at the siege of Lachish in 701 BC. More sophisticated devices were developed by the Romans which had iron boxes and tubes which were filled with incendiary substances and attached to arrows or spears. These arrows needed to be fired from loose bows, since swift flight extinguished the flame; spears could be launched by hand or throwing machine.

Flaming arrows and crossbow bolts were used throughout the period. 15th Century writer Gutierre Diaz de Gamez witnessed a Spanish attack on the Moorish town of Oran in 1404 and later described how "During the most part of the night, the galleys did not cease from firing bolts and quarrels dipped in tar into the town, which is near the sea. The noise and the cries which came from the town were very great by reason of the havoc that was wrought."

A 2 m (2.2 yd) long iron crossbow-bolt probably designed to carry a fire cartridge was found in a 13th-14th century castle in Vladimir, Eastern Russia. Such large machine-thrown bolts were ideal for incendiary weapons. The Mongols used an "ox-bow" machine to throw bolts which had been dipped in burning pitch, with a range of 2500 paces.

Anna Comnena records that at the 1091 Battle of Levunium, lighted torches were fixed to spears.

The Chinese Song Dynasty created fire arrows - rockets attached to arrows and launched in mass through platforms, and later created rockets such as the huo long chu shui, a multistage rocket used in naval combat. Primitive rockets made from bamboo and leather were used by the Mongols, under Genghis Khan, but were inaccurate. However, the Fatamids used "Chinese arrows" from the 11th Century, which probably included saltpetre. The Mamluks experimented with a rocket-powered weapon described as "an egg which moves itself and turns."

Depiction of Greek fire in the late 11th century Madrid Skylitzes manuscript.

Greek fire

Greek fire was one of the most effective thermal devices, although it was extremely dangerous for the users. A combustible liquid, it could be shot from siphons or catapults, and it burst into flames on impact. First developed by the Byzantines in the 7th century, it was later used by the Turks during the Crusades, and was probably first used in Western Europe in the 12th century. Early experiments by the Byzantines in the 6th century used a mixture of sulfur and oil, which would have been terrifying if not destructive. Various versions seem to have existed, and the recipes were frequently kept secret; experts today still debate the exact composition, although some recipes are known. It probably had regional variations; the Islamic derivative was known as "naft" and had a petroleum base, with sulfur; the Persian word for "petroleum" is نفت (*naft*).

The combustible liquid could be shot from catapults, and would burst into flames on impact. Siphons, frequently of copper, were also developed, first appearing in the 10th and 11th centuries. The siphons could shoot a blazing stream, which a 10th century Mesopotamian source claimed could engulf twelve men. Mardi bin Ali al-Tarsusi, who wrote a military manual for Saladin in the 12th century, suggested that "naft" could be placed inside blown eggshells, which could be thrown from horseback. From the 12th century, mouth-blown tubes were developed for use in mines.

Similar petroleum and bitumen-based incendiary mixtures had been known for centuries before the invention of Greek fire, but this new recipe created a blaze which was extremely difficult to extinguish. It burned on water, and was used effectively in naval warfare, although it was primarily an anti-personnel weapon rather than a ship-burner. It remained effective at sea even after its use had declined on land after the 13th century.

The Greek fire recipes continued to be developed over the centuries, and by the High Middle Ages was much more sophisticated than the early versions. Saltpetre (also called "Chinese salt") was added to the mixture in the Islamic world, and China developed a dry saltpetre mixture in the 12th century, which eventually became gunpowder.

Hot oil

Oil of various kinds could be heated to high temperatures and poured over enemy, although, since it was extremely expensive, its use was limited, both in frequency and quantity. Moreover, it could be dangerous and volatile. Since the smoke point of oil is lower than its boiling point, the oil was only heated and not boiled.

Pouring-oil was used in a number of historic battles, and Josephus described its use at Jotapata in AD 67, saying "the oil did easily run down the whole body from head to foot, under their entire armour, and fed upon their flesh like flame itself."

Oil was usually used to create incendiary devices. The Roman-Byzantine armies of the 6th century created "fire-pots", oil-based incendiary weapons which could be launched by hand or with ballistae. During the siege at Montreuil-en-Bellay in 1147, a mixture of oils from nuts, cannabis and flax, was heated in iron containers, launched by mangonel, and burst into flames on impact. The Chinese made early grenades out of oil-soaked hemp and cotton, which were ignited and thrown by mangonels.

Another use of oil can be seen in the naval battle of La Rochelle during the Hundred Years' War; the Castilians sprayed oil on the decks of English ships then ignited it by shooting flaming arrows down.

" They built copper and iron shields, put sand into them, and heated them over hot fire so the sand became red-hot. By means of some mechanism they threw this sand at those who had fought bravest and subjected their victims to most severe suffering. The sand penetrated through the armour into the shirts, burned the body, and it could not be helped [...] they died, going mad with horrible pain, in sufferings piteous and unquenchable. "

—*Diodorus Siculus, on the 4th century BC Siege of Tyre*

Water, sand and other heated missiles

Hot oil was considerably less common than boiling water or heated sand, which were cheap and extremely effective; even "dust from the street" could be used. These would penetrate armour and cause terrible burns. Sand, especially, could work its way through very small gaps in armour. The Phoenicians at the Siege of Tyre in 332 BC dropped burning sand down on the attacking Greeks, which got in behind the armour and burned the flesh. Such heated missiles have also been used in mining situations; the 1st century Roman writer Vitruvius describes a counter-mine dug above the attackers' gallery by defenders at the siege of Apollonia. Piercing the floor between the mines, the Apollonian defenders poured down boiling water, hot sand and hot pitch onto the heads of their enemy. Other mixtures were more innovative; the defenders at Chester in 918 boiled a mixture of water and ale in copper tubs and poured it over the Viking besiegers, causing their skin to peel off.

When Frederick I Babarossa besieged Crema, Italy in the 12th century, the defenders threw red-hot iron objects down on them.

Pitch, tar and resin

Burning pitch was used on occasion; the Mongols were known to fire containers of burning tar during sieges using catapults and trebuchets. Wheels could be covered in pitch, set alight and rolled along; this technique was commonly used during the Crusades. The besieged Carthaginians in Motya, 398 BC, set alight the siege engines of the attacking Syracusan forces under Dionysius I by dropping burning charred logs and resin-soaked oakum; however, the Syracusans were able to put out the fires.

Pitch was a base ingredient in many incendiary devices throughout the period. The Boeotians developed a fire machine, which they used against the Athenian wooden fortifications during the Battle of Delium in 424 BC. A cauldron of burning coals, pitch and sulfur was suspended at one end of a hollowed-out log and bellows were fixed to the other end. A similar mixture was used 900 years later by the Scots, when they dropped bales of wood, tar and sulfur by crane onto the English "sow" (a large protective shield covering the battering ram) at the 1319 siege of Ber-

Animal products

At the 1215 siege of Rochester Castle, King John ordered the fat from 40 pigs be used to set fire to the new mines beneath the keep, which caused it to collapse, a cheap and effective technique he used in preference to the more complicated mixture of sulfur, tallow, gum, pitch and quicksilver he had used in France the previous year. Animal fat was not uncommon as an accelerant; in the 13th century French sortie-parties would often be equipped with animal fat, straw and flax to use as fuel when setting fires amongst enemy siege engines.

There were some intriguing uses of animal products; during the Siege of Paris in 886 AD, the Franks dropped bucket-loads of a hot mixture of pitch (or oil), wax and fish on the attacking Vikings; the mixture got under the armour and stuck to the skin. Konrad Kyeser's *Bellifortis* of 1405 describes a poisonous mixture of sulfur, tar and horses' hooves. Other incendiary ingredients included egg yolks, and pigeon and sheep droppings. Live insects were also used, to sting the enemy. 4th century BC writer Aeneas Tacticus suggested defenders should let wasps and bees into enemy mines, and jars of scorpions were sometimes fired during early bombardment in naval battles.

In 189 BC Ambracia was besieged by the Romans, who dug mines under the walls. The defenders filled a clay jar with chicken feathers, which they then lit, using bellows to blow the acrid smoke down the tunnel; unable to approach the pot due to defensive spears, the Romans were forced to abandon their workings.

Quicklime, sulfur and smoke

The 15th-century engineer Taccola recommended quicklime, although its use went back to ancient times, and might well have been a component of Greek fire. Quicklime reacts violently with water, and can cause blindness and burns. While quicklime was used in some naval battles, it does not appear to have been standard issue on board ships, due to the danger of the quicklime blowing back and burning the user.

Other substances smoked rather than flamed. Sacks of burning sulfur were effective at clearing enemy mines due to the toxic smoke produced. Any smoke could be used in small confines; the Greek military writer Aeneas Tacticus recommended burning wood and straw to drive out enemy sappers by the smoke.

Gunpowder and cannon

Siege of Orleans in 1428 (Vigiles de Charles VII, 15th century)

The discovery of gunpowder was probably the product of centuries of alchemical experimentation. Saltpetre was known to the Chinese by the mid-1st century AD and there is strong evidence of the use of saltpetre and sulfur in various largely medicinal combinations. The impetus for the development of gunpowder weapons in China was increasing encroachment by tribes on its borders. In a separate development in Europe, Roger Bacon invented gunpowder in the mid-13th century, although the mixture was not very effective. The composition of gunpowder varied throughout the period, and did not settle into the current ratios of saltpetre, sulfur and coal until the 17th century.

The earliest known formula for gunpowder can be found in a Chinese work dating probably from the 9th century. The Chinese wasted little time in applying it to warfare, and they produced a variety of gunpowder weapons, including flamethrowers, rockets, bombs, and mines, before inventing firearms.

The years 904–906 saw the use of incendiary projectiles called 'flying fires' (*fei-kuo*). Needham (1986) argues that gunpowder was first used in warfare in China in 919 as a fuse for the ignition of another incendiary, Greek fire. Initially, gunpowder mixtures were utilised through traditional engines and throwing mechanisms; containers and grenades were thrown by mangonels and trebuchets, and explosive rockets and arrows were developed, along with gunpowder flamethrowers.

Like firearms, cannon are a descendant of the fire-lance, a gunpowder-filled tube used as a flamethrower; shrapnel-like material was sometimes placed in the barrel so that it would fly out together with the flames. In due course, the proportion of saltpeter in the propellant was increased to increase its explosive power. To better withstand that explosive power, the paper and bamboo of which fire-lance barrels were originally made came to be replaced by metal. And to take full advantage of that power, the shrapnel came to be replaced by projectiles whose size and shape filled the barrel more closely. With this, we have the three basic features of the gun: a barrel made of metal, high-nitrate gunpowder, and a projectile which totally occludes the muzzle so that the powder charge exerts its full potential in propellant effect.

Firearms remained in use in China throughout the following centuries. Meanwhile, gunpowder and firearms spread elsewhere very quickly. Gunpowder seems to have been widely known by the 13th century. The Europeans, Arabs, and Koreans all obtained firearms in the 14th century. The Turks, Iranians, and Indians all got firearms no later than the 15th century, in each case directly or indirectly from the Europeans. The Japanese did not acquire firearms until the 16th century, and then from the Portuguese rather than the Chinese.

In 1326, the earliest known European picture of a gun appeared in a treatise entitled "Of the Majesty, Wisdom and Prudence of Kings." On February 11 of that same year, the Signoria of Florence appointed two officers to obtain *canones de mettallo* and ammunition for the town's defense. A reference from 1331 describes an attack mounted by two Germanic knights on Cividale del Friuli, using gunpowder weapons of some sort. Cannon were first used by the Muslims at Alicante in 1331, or Algeciras in 1343. The French raiding party that sacked and burned Southampton in 1338 brought with them a ribaudequin and 48 bolts (but only 3 pounds of gunpowder). The Battle of Crécy in 1346 was one of the first in Europe where cannons were used.

However, early cannon were not very effective, the main benefits being psychological, frightening men and horses. Short barrelled, large-calibre "bombards" were used up until the late 15th century in Europe, during which period they grew increasingly larger. In the mid-15th century, mortars also appeared. Various smaller weapons also existed, including the *serpentine*, *ribaudequin* and *cropaudin*. The powder was of poor quality and was used in small quantities – to prevent explosion of the barrel – so the effective range of these cannon was rarely more than 200–250m.

The barrels of the cannon were forged or cast, and each gun generally differed in calibre and length. Early powder resembled a paste, and tended to burn slowly. Its composition varied in different geographical areas, the powder of Europe being quite different to that used in the Islamic world. The projectiles used were generally stone balls for bombards and mortars. Forged iron balls were used in smaller-calibre cannon, and coated with lead to make them smooth. From the 15th century, cast iron balls were used, which caused great destruction. As they were denser than stone, even small balls could be destructive. Thus, cannon became smaller in calibre, and longer-barrels increased the range.

Later development

The use of incendiary devices had decreased by the 14th century, perhaps due to the increasingly economic realities of war where it became increasingly important that captured castles and towns were undamaged. Moreover, fewer wooden engines and structures were employed in the battlefield after the late 13th century, perhaps because of the prior success of the incendiary weapons at destroying them.

While the incidence of use dropped, towards the latter end of the Middle Ages the incendiary devices became more sophisticated, and the principle of wielding fire with sword remained present throughout the Early Modern and Modern periods; improving technology merely allowed the process to become more efficient.

Burned-out buildings in Hamburg after the 1943 Allied incendiary attacks.

The principle of fire and sword

Fire itself remained a part of warfare. In his reminisces of the Peninsular War (1807–1814), a British soldier recorded that the French soldiers would "regularly burn to the ground every place they pass through. In following them we find each town and village a heap of smoking ruins." During World War I, Leuven, in Belgium was "looted and burned in medieval fashion", when German soldiers set fire to much of the town, destroying the library and other cultural buildings, and causing outrage around the world. Yet the tactic was not dispensed with. In World War II, fire-bombing with incendiary bombs was carried out by the Germans against Britain during the Blitz, and by the Allies against Germany and Japan. After one heavy raid on Tokyo in March 1945, the resulting firestorms destroyed a quarter of the predominately wooden buildings. Much as the Ancient Greeks before them, it was a strategy of devastation. Fire has continued to be used as a destructive measure in warfare. During the 1991–1992 Gulf War, Iraq set fire to three-quarters of Kuwait's oil wells.

Fire remained an extremely successful weapon. During naval warfare of the Napoleonic wars, "the one thing most likely to destroy a ship was fire". Sometimes the fires were merely a side effect of weapon technology. Early firearms proved incendiary in their use and could start fires. During the Peninsular War, both Talavera and Salamanca battlefields were wracked by tremendous grassfires, first started by the guns. At the Battle of Trafalgar, 1805, the French ship *Achille* caught fire when musket-flashes from her own men's guns set fire to the tar and grease on the sail rigging; the ship eventually exploded.

Smoke screens have continued to be used by attackers and defenders as a means of sowing confusion and hiding movements. During naval battles in the 18–19th centuries, shots were sometimes fired early so a defensive screen was erected before the ships converged, to spoil the aim of the enemy.

Development and continued use of weapons

The major development of weapons in the early modern and modern periods occurred with firearms, which became progressively more efficient. Gunpowder settled into its standard ratio in the 17th century, and general ballistic technology improved. Initially, iron round shot replaced the earlier stone balls for cannon then, latterly, different types of shot were invented.

A carcass was a hollow projectile usually formed either by an iron cage of ribs joining two small rings or a cast iron ball with a number of holes. A carcass was so named because the iron cage was thought to resemble the ribs of a body. A carcass was filled with a highly flammable mixture. Carcasses were used for the first time by the French under Louis XIV in 1672.

For short range use against personnel, canister and the smaller naval grapeshot were popular during the 19th century; it comprised smaller iron or lead pellets contained within a case or bag, which scattered on explosion. In 1784, Lt Henry Shrapnel invented a spherical case-shot, which was later named after him. The case was a hollow iron sphere which was filled with musket balls and was detonated by a gunpowder charge. Shot fired from cannon could be so hot that it scorched or set fire to materials that it brushed.

A flame tank at Iwo Jima, World War II.

The incendiary liquids of the ancient and medieval periods were also developed, and have their modern equivalents. World War I saw the development of the flamethrower, a modern version of the Byzantine siphons, which used gas under pressure to squirt a mixture of inflammable oil and petrol, ignited by a burning taper. Similarly, the carcass projectile found new use in the Livens Projector, a primitive mortar that could throw a large canister of inflammable liquid (it was soon used for poison gas instead).

Technology improved throughout the 20th century, and the latter half saw the development and use of napalm, an incendiary liquid formed in part from naphtha, which was the main ingredient of the Arabic "naft".

Flames continued to be used for defensive light until artificial lights were developed. At the Siege of Badajoz in 1812, the French defenders flung down burning "carcasses" of straw so that the attacking British might be seen. Like the sieges of old, the British were met by incendiary weapons, but now these took the form of explosive grenades, mines and powder barrels as well as the enemy's guns.

Specific weapons from the ancient and medieval periods continued to develop, and many have modern equivalents. Rocket technology, originally trialled by the Mongols, Indians and the Chinese, amongst others, was improved by the 19th century; one example was the incendiary Congreve rocket, which had a tail, a fuse, and a powder charge (saltpetre, sulfur and carbon) inside a hollow shell. Grenades continued to develop, although still retaining some aspects of their medieval equivalents. The grenades carried on board Royal Navy ships in the late 18th century and early 19th century were constructed from hollow cast iron, filled with gunpowder; the fuse was a hollow wooden tube filled with combustible material. During World War I, grenades were still occasionally launched by ballistae.

The use of some weapons continued with little change. The Koreans used fire arrows against the Japanese at the Battle of Hansan Island in 1592. At Trafalgar, in 1805, the British ship *Tonnant* shot wads covered in sulfur, which set fire to the *Algésiras*. Fireships were used in later periods. In 1588, the English sent fireships loaded with gunpowder, pitch and tar amongst the anchored Spanish Armada; the Spanish fleet broke formation, setting them up for the later battle. The last battle under sail was the Battle of Navarino (1827), part of the Greek War of Independence, during which fireships were utilised by the Turks.

Chemical warfare had been experimented with during the early period with sulfur, quicklime (calcium oxide), and others, and developments continued. World War I saw many gases used, including the extremely effective sulfur mustard (mustard gas).

See also
- Scorched earth
- Boiling to death

Notes

References
- Adkins, Roy (2004). *Trafalgar: The Biography of a Battle*. London: Little, Brown. ISBN 0316715110.
- Bennet, Matthew; Bradbury, Jim; DeVries, Kelly; Dickie, Iain; Jestice, Phyllis G. (2005). *Fighting Techniques of the Medieval World: AD 500-AD 1500*. London: Amber Books. ISBN 1862272999.
- Bluth, BJ (2001). *Marching with Sharpe*. London: HarperCollins. ISBN 0004145372.
- Bradbury, Jim (1992). *The Medieval Siege*. Boydell & Brewer. ISBN 0851153577.
- Bradbury, Jim (2004). *The Routledge Companion to Medieval Warfare*. London: Routledge. ISBN 0415221269.
- Bryant, Arthur (1950). *The Age of Elegance: 1812–1822*. London: Collins.
- Buchanan, Brenda J (2006). *Gunpowder, Explosives and the State: A Technological History*. Ashgate.
- Carey, Brian Todd; Allfree, Joshua B; Cairns, John (2006). *Warfare in the Medieval World*. Pen & Sword Military. ISBN 1844153398.
- Cartledge, Paul (2004). *Alexander the Great: The Hunt for a New Past*. London: Macmillan. ISBN 1405032928.
- Chase, Kenneth (2003). *Firearms: A Global History to 1700*. Cambridge University Press.
- Crosby, Alfred W. (2002). *Throwing Fire: Projectile Technology Through History*. Cambridge University Press.
- Diaz de Gamez, Gutierre; Evans, Joan (trans.) (2004). *The Unconquered Knight: a Chronicle of the Deeds of Don Pero Niño, Count of Buelna*. Boydell Press. ISBN 1843831015.
- Grant, R.G. (2005). *Battle: a Visual Journey Through 5000 Years of Combat*. London: Dorling Kindersley. ISBN 1405311002.
- Haythornthwaite, Philip J. (1992). *The World War One Source Book*. London: Cassell. ISBN 1854091026.
- Kaufmann, J.E.; Kaufmann, H.W. (2001). *The Medieval Fortress: Castles, Forts and Walled Cities of the Middle Ages*. Greenhill Books. ISBN 1853674559.
- Kelly, Jack (2004). *Gunpowder: Alchemy, Bombards, & Pyrotechnics: The History of the Explosive that Changed the World*. Basic Books.
- Matarasso, François (2000). *The*

English Castle. Caxton Editions. ISBN 1840672307.
- Needham, Joseph (1986). *Science & Civilisation in China: The Gunpowder Epic.* **7**. Cambridge University Press.
- Nicolle, David (1996). *Medieval Warfare Source Book: Christian Europe and its Neighbours.* Brockhampton Press. ISBN 1860198619.
- Nicolle, David (1995). *Medieval Warfare Source Book: Warfare in Western Christendom.* Brockhampton Press. ISBN 1860198899.
- Nossov, Konstantin (2006). *Ancient and Medieval Siege Weapons.* Spellmount. ISBN 186227343X.
- Ortzen, Len (1976). *Guns at Sea: The World's Great Naval Battles.* London: Weidenfeld and Nicolson. ISBN 0297771620.
- Prestwich, Michael (1996). *Armies and Warfare in the Middle Ages: The English Experience.* New Haven: Yale University Press. ISBN 0300076630.
- Traquir, Peter (1998). *Freedom's Sword: Scotland's Wars of Independence.* London: HarperCollins. ISBN 0004720792.

Source http://en.wikipedia.org/wiki/Early_thermal_weapons

Greek fire

Byzantine ship using Greek fire in the late 11th century. Madrid Skylitzes manuscript.

Greek fire was an incendiary weapon used by the Byzantine Empire. The Byzantines typically used it in naval battles to great effect as it could continue burning even under water.

It provided a technological advantage, and was responsible for many key Byzantine military victories, most notably the salvation of Constantinople from two Arab sieges, thus securing the Empire's survival.

The impression made by Greek fire on the European Crusaders was such that the name was applied to any sort of incendiary weapon, including those used by Arabs, the Chinese, and the Mongols. These, however, were different mixtures and not the Byzantine formula, which was a closely guarded state secret, whose composition has now been lost. As a result, its ingredients are a much debated topic, with proposals including naphtha, quicklime, sulphur, and niter. What set the Byzantine usage of incendiary mixtures apart was their use of pressurized siphons to project the liquid onto the enemy.

Although the term "Greek fire" has been general in English and most other languages since the Crusades, in the original Byzantine sources it is called by a variety of names, such as "sea fire" (Greek: πῦρ θαλάσσιον), "Roman fire" (πῦρ ῥωμαϊκόν), "war fire" (πολεμικὸν πῦρ), "liquid fire" (ὑγρὸν πῦρ), or "processed fire" (πῦρ σκευαστόν).

History

Incendiary and flaming weapons were used in warfare for centuries prior to the invention of Greek fire. They included a number of sulphur-, petroleum- and bitumen-based mixtures. Incendiary arrows and pots containing combustible substances were used as early as the 9th century BC by the Assyrians, and were extensively used in the Greco-Roman world as well.

Furthermore, Thucydides mentions the use of tubed flamethrowers in the siege of Delium in 424 BC. In naval warfare, the fleet of the Byzantine Emperor Anastasius I (r. 491–518) is recorded by the chronicler John Malalas as having utilized a sulphur-based mixture to defeat the revolt of Vitalian in AD 515, following the advice of a philosopher from Athens called Proclus. Chronicle of Theophanes the Confessor, *Annus Mundi* 6165

Greek fire proper, however, was invented in ca. 672, and is ascribed by the chronicler Theophanes to Kallinikos, an architect from Heliopolis in the former province of Phoenice, by then overrun by the Muslim conquests. The historicity and exact chronology of this account is open to question: Theophanes reports the use of fire-carrying and siphon-equipped ships by the Byzantines a couple of years before the supposed arrival of Kallinikos at Constantinople. If this is not due to chronological confusion of the events of the siege, it may suggest that Kallinikos merely introduced an improved version of an established weapon. The historian James Partington further thinks it likely that Greek fire was not in fact the discovery of any single person, but "invented by chemists in Constantinople who had inherited the discoveries of the Alexandrian chemical school". Indeed, the 11th-century chronicler George Kedrenos records that Kallinikos came from Heliopolis in Egypt, but most scholars reject this as an error. Kedrenos also records the story, considered rather implausible, that Kallinikos' descendants, a family called *"Lampros"* ("Brilliant"), kept the secret of the fire's manufacture, and continued doing so to his day.

The invention of Greek fire came at a critical moment in the Byzantine Empire's history: weakened by its long wars with Sassanid Persia, the Byzantines had been unable to effectively resist the onslaught of the Muslim conquests. Within a generation, Syria, Palestine and Egypt had fallen to the Arabs, who in ca. 672 set out to conquer the imperial capital of Constantinople. The Greek fire was utilized to great effect against the Muslim fleets, helping to repel the Muslims at the first and second Arab sieges of the city. Records of its use in later naval battles against the Saracens are more sporadic, but it did secure a number of victories, especially in the phase of Byzantine expansion in the late 9th and early 10th centuries. Utilisation of the substance was prominent in Byzantine civil wars, chiefly the revolt of the thematic fleets in 727 and the large-scale rebellion led by Thomas the Slav in 821–823. In both cases, the rebel fleets were defeated by the Constantinopolitan Imperial Fleet through the use of Greek fire. The Byzantines also used the weapon to devastating effect against the various Rus' raids to the Bosporus, especially those of 941 and 1043, as well as during the Bulgarian war of 970–971, when the fire-carrying Byzantine ships blockaded the Danube.

The importance placed on Greek fire during the Empire's struggle against the Arabs would lead to its discovery being ascribed to divine intervention. The Emperor Constantine Porphyrogennetos (r. 945–959), in his book *De Administrando Imperio*, admonishes his son and heir, Romanos II (r. 959–963), to never reveal the secrets of its construction, as it was "shown and revealed by an angel to the great and holy first Christian emperor Constantine" and that the angel bound him "not to prepare this fire but for Christians, and only in the imperial city". As a warning, he adds that one official, who was bribed into handing some of it over to the Empire's enemies, was struck down by a "flame from heaven" as he was about to enter a church. As the latter incident demonstrates, the Byzantines could not avoid capture of their precious secret weapon: the Arabs captured at least one fireship intact in 827, and the Bulgars captured several siphons and much of the substance itself in 812/814. This, however, was apparently not enough to allow their enemies to copy it (see below). The Arabs for instance employed a variety of incendiary substances similar to the Byzantine weapon, but they were never able to copy the Byzantine method of deployment by siphon, and used catapults and grenades instead.

Greek fire continued to be mentioned during the 12th century, and Anna Komnene gives a vivid description of its use in a – possibly fictional – naval battle against the Pisans in 1099. However, although the use of hastily improvised fireships is mentioned during the 1203 siege of Constantinople by the Fourth Crusade, no report confirms the use of the actual Greek fire, which had apparently fallen out of use, either because its secrets were forgotten, or because the Byzantines had lost access to the areas – the Caucasus and the eastern coast of the Black Sea – where the primary ingredients were to be found.

Manufacture

General characteristics

As Constantine Porphyrogennetos' warnings show, the ingredients and the processes of manufacture and deployment of Greek fire were extremely carefully guarded military secrets. So strict was the secrecy that the composition of Greek fire was lost forever and remains a source of speculation to this day. Consequently, the "mystery" of the formula has long dominated the research into Greek fire. Despite this almost exclusive focus, however, Greek fire is best understood as a complete weapon system of many components, all of which were needed to operate together to render it effective. This comprised not only the formula of its composition, but also the specialized dromons, the device used to prepare the substance by heating and pressurizing it, the siphon projecting it, and the special training of the *siphōnarioi* who used it. Knowledge of the whole system was highly compartmentalised, with operators and technicians aware of the secrets of only one component, ensuring that no enemy could gain knowledge of it in its entirety. This accounts for the fact that when the Bulgarians took Mesembria and Debeltos in 814, they captured 36 siphons and even quantities of the substance itself, but were unable to make any use of them.

The information available on Greek fire is exclusively indirect, based on references in the Byzantine military manuals and a number of secondary historical sources such as Anna Komnene and Western European chroniclers, which however are often inaccurate. In her *Alexiad*, Anna Komnene provides a description of an incendiary weapon, which was used by the Byzantine garrison of Dyrrhachium in 1108 against the Normans. It is often regarded as an at least partial "recipe" for Greek fire: "This fire is made by the following arts. From the pine and the certain such evergreen trees inflammable resin is collected. This is rubbed with sulphur and put into tubes of reed, and is blown by men using it with violent and continuous breath. Then in this manner it meets the fire on the tip and catches light and falls like a fiery whirlwind on the faces of the enemies."

At the same time, the reports by Western chroniclers of the famed *ignis graecus* are largely unreliable, since they apply the name to any and all sorts of incendiary substances.

In attempting to reconstruct the Greek fire system, the concrete evidence, as it emerges from the contemporary literary references, provides the following characteristics:

- It burned on water, and, according to some interpretations, was ignited by water. In addition, as numerous writers testify, it could be extinguished only by a few substances, such as sand, which deprived it of oxygen, strong vinegar, or old urine, presumably by some sort of chemical reaction.
- It was a liquid substance, and not some sort of projectile, as verified both by descriptions and the very name "liquid fire".
- At sea, it was usually ejected from siphons, although earthenware pots or grenades filled with it or similar substances were also used.
- The discharge of Greek fire was accompanied by "thunder" and "much smoke".

Theories on composition

The first and, for a long time, most popular theory regarding the composition of Greek fire held that its chief ingredient was saltpeter, making it an early form of gunpowder. This argument was based on the "thunder and smoke" description, as well as on the distance the flame could be projected from a siphon, which suggested an explosive discharge. From the times of Isaac Vossius, several scholars adhered to this position, most notably the so-called

"French school" during the 19th century, which included the famous chemist Marcellin Berthelot. This view has been rejected since, as saltpeter does not appear to have been used in warfare in Europe or the Middle East before the 13th century, and is totally absent from the accounts of the Arabs, the foremost chemists of the Mediterranean world, before the same period. In addition, the nature of the proposed mixture would have been radically different from the siphon-projected substance described by Byzantine sources.

A second view, based on the fact that Greek fire was inextinguishable by water – rather, some sources suggest that pouring water on it intensified the flames – suggested that its destructive power was the result of the explosive reaction between water and quicklime. Although quicklime was certainly known and used by the Byzantines and the Arabs in warfare, the theory is refuted by literary and empirical evidence. A quicklime-based substance would have to come in contact with water to ignite, while Emperor Leo's *Tactica* indicate that Greek fire was often poured directly on the decks of enemy ships, although admittedly, decks were kept wet due to lack of sealants. Likewise, Leo prescribes the use of grenades, which further reinforces the view that contact with water was not necessary for the substance's ignition. Furthermore, C. Zenghelis pointed out that, based on experiments, the actual result of the water-quicklime reaction would be negligible in the open sea. Another similar proposition suggested that Kallinikos had in fact discovered calcium phosphide. On contact with water, calcium phosphide releases phosphine, which ignites spontaneously. However, extensive experiments with it also failed to reproduce the described intensity of Greek fire.

Although the presence of either quicklime or saltpeter in the mixture cannot be entirely excluded, they were consequently not the primary ingredient. Most modern scholars agree that the actual Greek fire was based on petroleum, either crude or refined; comparable to modern napalm. The Byzantines had easy access to crude oil from the naturally occurring wells around the Black Sea (e.g., the wells around Tmutorakan noted by Constantine Porphyrogennetos) or in various locations throughout the Middle East. An alternate name for Greek fire was "Median fire" (μηδικὸν πῦρ), and the 6th-century historian Procopius, records that crude oil, which was called *naphtha* (in Greek νάφθα, *naphtha*, from Middle Persian نفت (*naft*)) by the Persians, was known to the Greeks as "Median oil" (μηδικὸν ἔλαιον). This seems to corroborate the use of naphtha as a basic ingredient of Greek fire. There is also a surviving 9th-century Latin text, preserved at Wolfenbüttel in Germany, which mentions the ingredients of what appears to be Greek fire and the operation of the siphons used to project it. Although the text contains some inaccuracies, it clearly identifies the main component as naphtha. Resins were probably added as a thickener (the *Praecepta Militaria* refer to the substance as πῦρ κολλητικόν, "sticky fire"), and to increase the duration and intensity of the flame.

A 12th-century treatise prepared by Mardi bin Ali al-Tarsusi for Saladin records an Arab version of Greek fire, called *naft*, which also had a petroleum base, with sulphur and various resins added. Any direct relation however with the Byzantine formula is very unlikely.

Methods of deployment

Use of a *cheirosiphōn* ("hand-siphon"), a portable flamethrower, used from atop a flying bridge against a castle. Illumination from the *Poliorcetica* of Hero of Byzantium.

The chief method of deployment of Greek fire, which sets it apart from similar substances, was its projection through a tube (*siphōn*), for use aboard ships or in sieges. Portable projectors (*cheirosiphōnes*) were also invented, reputedly by Emperor Leo VI. The Byzantine military manuals also mention that jars (*kytrai* or *tzykalia*) filled with Greek fire and caltrops wrapped with tow and soaked in the substance were thrown by catapults, while pivoting cranes (*gerania*) were employed to pour it upon enemy ships. The *cheirosiphōnes* especially were prescribed for use at land and in sieges, both against siege machines and against defenders on the walls, by several 10th-century military authors, and their use is depicted in the *Poliorcetica* of Hero of Byzantium. The Byzantine dromons usually had a *siphōn* installed on their prow under the forecastle, but additional devices could also on occasion be placed elsewhere on the ship. Thus in 941, when the Byzantines were facing the vastly more numerous Rus' fleet, siphons were placed also amidships and even astern.

Siphon projectors

The use of siphons is amply attested in the contemporary sources. Anna Komnene gives this account of beast-shaped Greek fire projectors being mounted to the bow of warships: "As he [the Emperor Alexios I] knew that the Pisans were skilled in sea warfare and dreaded a battle with them, on the prow of each ship he had a head fixed of a lion or other land-animal, made in brass or iron with the mouth open and then gilded over, so that their mere aspect was terrifying. And the fire which was to be directed against the enemy through tubes he made to pass through the mouths of the beasts, so that it seemed as if the lions and the other similar monsters were vomiting the fire."

Some sources provide more information on the composition and function of the whole mechanism. The Wolfenbüttel manuscript in particular provides the following description:

"...having built a furnace right at the front of the ship, they set on it a copper vessel full of these things, having put fire underneath. And one of them, having made a bronze tube similar to that which the rustics call a *squitiatoria*, "squirt", with which boys play, they spray [it] at the enemy."

Another, possibly first-hand, account of the use of Greek fire comes from the 11th-century *Yngvars saga víðförla*, where the Viking Ingvar the Far-Travelled faces ships equipped with Greek fire siphons:

"[They] began blowing with smiths' bellows at a furnace in which there was fire and there came from it a great din. There stood there also a brass [or bronze] tube and from it flew much fire against one ship, and it burned up in a short time so that all of it became white ashes..."

The account, albeit embellished, corresponds with many of the characteristics of Greek fire known from other sources, such as a loud roar that accompanied its discharge. These two texts are also the only two sources that explicitly mention that the substance was heated over a furnace before being discharged; although the validity of this information is open to question, modern reconstructions have relied upon them.

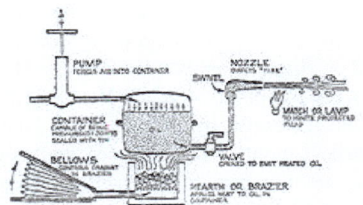

Proposed reconstruction of the Greek fire mechanism by Haldon and Byrne

Based on these descriptions and the Byzantine sources, John Haldon and Maurice Byrne reconstructed the entire apparatus as consisting of three main components: a bronze pump (the σίφων, *siphōn* proper), which was used to pressurize the oil; a brazier, used to heat the oil (πρόπυρον, *propyron*, "pre-heater"); and the nozzle, which was covered in bronze and mounted on a swivel (στρεπτόν, *strepton*). The brazier, burning a match of linen or flax that produced intense heat and the characteristic thick smoke, was used to heat oil and the other ingredients in an airtight tank above it, a process that also helped to dissolve the resins into a fluid mixture. The substance was pressurized by the heat and the usage of a force pump. After it had reached the proper pressure, a valve connecting the tank with the swivel was opened and the mixture was discharged from its end, being ignited at its mouth by some source of flame. The intense heat of the flame made necessary the presence of heat shields made of iron (βουκόλια, *boukolia*), which are attested in the fleet inventories.

The whole process was fraught with danger, as the mounting pressure could easily make the heated oil explode, although there are no recorded circumstances of such accidents. In the experiments conducted by Haldon in 2002 for the episode *Fireship* of the television series *Machines Times Forgot*, even modern welding techniques failed to secure adequate insulation of the bronze tank under pressure. This led to the relocation of the pressure pump between the tank and the nozzle. The full-scale device built on this basis established the effectiveness of the mechanism's design, even with the simple materials and techniques available to the Byzantines. The experiment used crude oil mixed with wood resins, and achieved a flame of over 1 000 °C (1,830 °F) and an effective range of up to 15 meters (49 ft).

Hand-held siphons

Detail of hand-siphon.

The portable *cheirosiphōn* ("hand-siphon"), the earliest analogue to a modern flame-thrower, is extensively attested in the military documents of the 10th century, and recommended for use in both sea and land. They first appear in the *Tactica* of emperor Leo VI the Wise, who claims to have invented them. Subsequent authors continued to refer to the *cheirosiphōnes*, especially for use against siege towers, although Nikephoros II Phokas also advises their use in field armies, with the aim of disrupting the enemy formation. Although both Leo VI and Nikephoros Phokas claim that the substance used in the *cheirosiphōnes* was the same as in the static devices used on ships, they were manifestly different devices than their larger cousins. This led Haldon and Byrne to theorize that the device was fundamentally different, "a simple syringe [that] squirted both liquid fire (presumably unignited) and noxicus juices to repel enemy troops." Nevertheless, as the illustrations of Hero's *Poliorcetica* show, the hand-siphons too threw the ignited substance.

Grenades

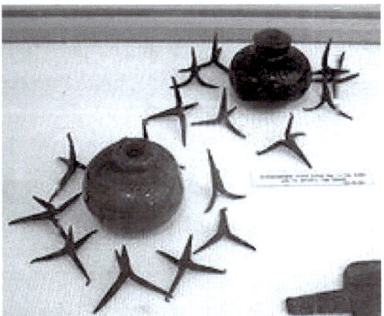

Clay grenades that were filled with Greek fire, 10th–12th centuries, National Historical Museum, Athens, Greece

In its earliest form, Greek fire was hurled onto enemy forces by firing a burning cloth-wrapped ball, perhaps containing a flask, using a form of light catapult, most probably a seaborne variant of the Roman light catapult or onager. These were capable of hurling light loads—around 6 to 9 kg (13 to 20 lb)—a distance of 350–450 m (383–492 yd). Later technological improvements in machining technology enabled the devising of a pump mechanism discharging a stream of burning fluid (flame thrower) at close ranges, devastating wooden ships in naval warfare. Such weapons were also very effective on land when used against besieging forces.

Effectiveness and countermeasures

Although the destructiveness of Greek fire is indisputable, it should not be seen as some sort of "wonder weapon", nor did it make the Byzantine navy invincible. It was not, in the words of naval historian John Pryor, a "ship-killer" comparable to the naval ram, which by then had fallen out of use. While Greek fire remained a potent weapon, its limitations were significant when compared to more traditional forms of artillery: in its siphon-deployed version, it had a limited range, and it could be used safely only in a calm sea and with favourable wind conditions. The enemy Muslim navies eventually adapted themselves to it, by staying out of its effective range and devising methods of protection such as felt or hides soaked in vinegar.

Source   http://en.wikipedia.org/wiki/Greek_fire

Gunpowder artillery in the Middle Ages

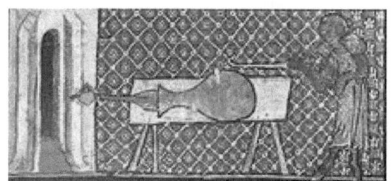

The earliest illustration of a European cannon, from around 1327.

Artillery in the Middle Ages primarily consisted of the introduction of the cannon, large tubular firearms designed to fire a heavy projectile over a long distance. They were used in China, Europe and the Middle East during the period.

Although gunpowder was known in Europe during the High Middle Ages, it was not until the Late Middle Ages that cannons were widely developed. The first cannons in Europe were probably used in Iberia, during the Islamic wars against the Christians in the 13th century; their use was also first documented in the Middle East around this time. English cannons first appeared in 1327, and later saw more general use during the Hundred Years' War, when primitive cannons were engaged at the Battle of Crécy in 1346. By the end of the 14th century, the use of cannons was also recorded in Russia, Byzantium and the Ottoman Empire.

The earliest medieval cannon, the *pot-de-fer*, had bulbous, vase-like shape, and was used more for psychological effect than for causing physical damage. The later culverin was transitional between the handgun and the full cannon, and was used as an anti-personnel weapon. During the 15th century, cannon advanced significantly, so that bombards were effective siege engines. Towards the end of the period, cannon gradually replaced siege engines—among other forms of aging weaponry—on the battlefield.

The Middle English word *Canon* was derived from the Old Italian word *cannone*, meaning *large tube*, which came from Latin *canna*, meaning *cane* or *reed*. The Latinised word *canon* has been used for a gun since 1326 in Italy, and since 1418 in English. The word *Bombardum*, or "bombard", was earliest term used for "cannon", but from 1430 it came to refer only to the largest weapons.

The first documented battlefield use of gunpowder artillery took place on January 28, 1132, when Song General Han Shizhong used huochong to capture a city in Fujian. The world's earliest known cannon, dated 1282, was found in Mongol-held Manchuria. The first known illustration of a cannon is dated to 1326. In his 1341 poem, *The Iron Cannon Affair*, one of the first accounts of the use of gunpowder artillery in China, Xian Zhang wrote that a cannonball fired from an eruptor could "pierce the heart or belly when it strikes a man or horse, and can even transfix several persons at once."

Use in the Islamic world

The Arabs acquired knowledge of gunpowder some time after 1240, but before 1280, by which time Hasan al-Rammah had written, in Arabic, recipes for gunpowder, instructions for the purification of saltpeter, and descriptions of gunpowder incendiaries.

Ahmad Y. al-Hassan claims that the Battle of Ain Jalut in 1260 saw the Mamluks use against the Mongols in "the first cannon in history" gunpowder formulae which were almost identical with the ideal composition for explosive gunpowder, which he claims were not known in China or Europe until much later. However, Iqtidar Alam Khan states that it was invading Mongols who introduced gunpowder to the Islamic world and cites Mamluk antagonism towards early riflemen in their infantry as an example of how gunpowder weapons were not always met with open acceptance in the Middle East.

Al-Hassan interprets Ibn Khaldun as reporting the use of cannon as siege machines by the Marinid sultan Abu Yaqub Yusuf at the siege of Sijilmasa in 1274. Super-sized bombards were used by the troops of Mehmed II to capture Constantinople, in 1453. Urban, a Hungarian cannon engineer, is credited with the introduction of this cannon from Central Europe to the Ottoman realm. It could fire heavy stone balls a mile, and the sound of their blast could reportedly be heard from a distance of 10 miles (16 km). A piece of slightly later date (see pic) was cast in bronze and made in two parts: the chase and the breech, which, together, weighed 18.4 tonnes. The two parts were screwed together using levers to facilitate the work.

Use in Europe

In Europe, the first mention of gunpowder's composition in express terms appeared in Roger Bacon's "*De nullitate magiæ*" at Oxford, published in 1216. Later, in 1248, his "*Opus Maior*" describes a recipe for gunpowder and rec-

Roger Bacon described the first gunpowder in Europe.

ognized its military use:
We can, with saltpeter and other substances, compose artificially a fire that can be launched over long distances ... By only using a very small quantity of this material much light can be created accompanied by a horrible fracas. It is possible with it to destroy a town or an army ... In order to produce this artificial lightning and thunder it is necessary to take saltpeter, sulfur, and Luru Vopo Vir Can Utriet.

In 1250, the Norwegian *Konungs skuggsjá* mentioned, in its military chapter, the use of "coal and sulphur" as the best weapon for ship-to-ship combat.

Muslim and Christian Iberia

The Almohad dynasty of Al-Andalus used Moorish cannon defensively at the sieges of Seville, in 1248, and Niebla, in 1262. In reference to the siege to Alicante in 1331, the Spanish historian Zurita recorded a "new machine that caused great terror. It threw iron balls with fire." The Spanish historian Juan de Mariana recalled further use of cannon during the capture of Algeciras in 1342:
The besieged did great harm among the Christians with iron bullets they shot. This is the first time we find any mention of gunpowder and ball in our histories.

Juan de Mariana also relates that the English Earl of Derby and Earl of Salisbury had both participated in the siege of Algeciras, and they could have conceivably transferred the knowledge about the effectiveness of cannon to England.

The Iberian kings at the initial stages enlisted the help of Moorish experts:
The first artillery-masters on the Peninsula probably were Moors in Christian service. The king of Navarre had a Moor in his service in 1367 as *maestro de las guarniciones de artilleria*. The Morisques of Tudela at that time had fame for their capacity in *reparaciones de artilleria*.

Britain and France

A reconstruction of the *pot-de-fer* vase cannon that fired arrows.

Cannon seem to have been introduced to the Kingdom of England in the 14th century, and is mentioned as being in use against the Scots in 1327. The first metal cannon was the *pot-de-fer*, first depicted in an illuminated manuscript by Walter de Milamete, of 1327 that was presented to Edward III upon his accession to the English throne. The manuscript shows a four-legged stand supporting a "bulbous bottle", while the gunner stands well back, firing the charge with a red-hot iron bar. A bolt protrudes from the muzzle, but no wad is shown. Although illustrated in the treatise, no explanation or description was given.

This weapon, and others similar, were used by both the French and English during the Hundred Years' War (1337–1453), when cannon saw their first real use on the European battlefield. The cannon of the 14th century were still limited in many respects, as a modern historian summarises:
Early cannon were inferior in every respect to the great siege-engines: they were slow and small, they were limited... [in the 14th century] to firing bolts or 'garrots' and they had a very limited range. The weaknesses were due to limited technology: inability to forge or cast in one piece or make iron balls. They were probably as dangerous to their users as to the enemy and affected the morale of men (and horses) rather than damaged persons or buildings.

During the 1340s, cannon were still relatively rare, and were only used in small numbers by a few states. "Ribaldis" were first mentioned in the English Privy Wardrobe accounts during preparations for the Battle of Crécy between 1345 and 1346. These were believed to have shot large arrows and simple grapeshot, but they were so important they were directly controlled by the Royal Wardrobe. According to the contemporary chronicler Jean Froissart, the English cannon made "two or three discharges on the Genoese", which is taken to mean individual shots by two or three guns because of the time taken to reload such primitive artillery. The Florentine Giovanni Villani agreed that they were destructive on the field, though he also indicated that the guns continued to fire upon French cavalry later in the battle:
The English guns cast iron balls by means of fire... They made a noise like thunder and caused much loss in men and horses... The Genoese were continually hit by the archers and the gunners... [by the end of the battle] the whole plain was covered by men struck down by arrows and cannon balls.

Advances in the Late Middle Ages

Similar cannon to those used at Crécy appeared also at the Siege of Calais in the same year, and by the 1380s the "ribaudekin" clearly became mounted on wheels. Wheeled gun carriages became more commonplace by the end of the 15th century, and were more often cast in bronze, rather than banding iron sections together. There were still the logistical problems both of transporting and of operating the cannon, and as

The first Western image of a battle with cannon: the Siege of Orleans in 1429

many three dozen horses and oxen may have been required to move some of the great guns of the period.

Another small-bore cannon of the 14th century was the culverin, whose name derives from the snake-like handles attached to it. It was transitional between the handgun and the full cannon, and was used as an anti-personnel weapon. The culverin was forged of iron and fixed to a wooden stock, and usually placed on a rest for firing. Some of the loopholes in the gatehouse at Bodiam Castle appear to have been intended for culverin use.

15th century culveriners.

The culverin was also common in 15th century battles, particularly among Burgundian armies. As the smallest of medieval gunpowder weapons, it was relatively light and portable. It fired lead shot, which was inexpensive relative to other available materials. There was also the demi-culverin, which was smaller and had a bore of 4 inches (10 cm).

Considerable developments in the 15th century produced very effective "bombards" — an early form of battering cannon used against walls and towers. These were used both defensively and offensively. Bamburgh Castle, previously thought impregnable, was taken by bombards in 1464. The keep in Wark, Northumberland was described in 1517 as having five storeys "in each of which there were five great murder-holes, shot with great vaults of stone, except one stage which is of timber, so that great bombards can be shot from each of them." An example of a bombard was found in the moat of Bodiam Castle, and a replica is now kept inside.

Hand culverin (middle) with two small cannon, Europe, 15th century.

Artillery crews were generally recruited from the city hookers. The master gunner was usually the same person as the caster. In larger contingents, the master gunners had responsibility for the heavier artillery pieces, and were accompanied by their journeymen as well as smiths, carpenters, rope makers and carters. Smaller field pieces would be manned by trained volunteers. At the Battle of Flodden Field, each cannon had its crew of gunner, matrosses and drivers, and a group of "pioneers" were assigned to level to path ahead. Even with a level path, the gunpowder mixture used was unstable and could easily separate out into sulphur, saltpetre and charcoal during transport.

Once on site, they would be fired at ground level behind a hinged timber shutter, to provide some protection to the artillery crew. Timber wedges were used to control the barrel's elevation. The majority of medieval cannon were breechloaders, although there was still no effort to standardise calibres. The usual loading equipment consisted of a copper loading scoop, a ramrod, and a felt brush or "sponge". A bucket of water was always kept beside the cannon. Skins or cloths soaked in cold water could be used to cool down the barrel, while acids could also be added to the water to clean out the inside of the barrel. Hot coals were used to heat the shot or keep the wire primer going.

Some Scottish kings were very interested in the development of cannon, including the unfortunate James II, who was killed by the accidental explosion of one of his own cannon besieging Roxburgh Castle in 1460. Mons Meg, which dates from about the same time, is perhaps the most famous example of a Scottish cannon. James IV was Scotland's first Renaissance figure, who also had a fascination with cannon, both at land and at sea. By 1502, he was able to invest in a Scottish navy, which was to have a large number of cannon — his flagship, the *Great Michael*, was launched in 1511, with 36 great guns, 300 lesser pieces and 120 gunners.

Use in Eastern Europe

Tokhtamysh's Invasion of Russia, 1382. At this time, cannon and throwing-machines co-existed.

Russia

The first cannon appeared in Russia in the 1370-1380s, although initially their use was confined to sieges and the defence of fortresses. The first mention of cannon in Russian chronicles is of *tyufyaks*, small howitzer-type cannon that fired case-shot, used to defend Moscow against Tokhtamysh Khan in 1382. Cannon co-existed with throwing-machines until the mid-15th century, when they overtook the latter in terms of destructive power. In 1446, a Russian city fell to cannon fire for the first time, although its wall was not destroyed. The first stone wall to be destroyed in Russia by cannon fire came in 1481.

Byzantine and Ottoman Empires

During the 14th century, the Byzantine Empire began to accumulate its own cannon to face the Ottoman threat, starting with medium-sized cannon 3 feet (0.91 m) long and of 10" calibre. Only a few large bombards were under the Empire's control. The first definite use of artillery in the region was against the Ottoman siege of Constantinople in 1396, as the attackers did not yet have any gunpowder of their own. These loud Byzantine weapons, possibly operated by the Genoese or "Franks" of Galata, forced the Turks to withdraw.

The Ottomans had acquired their own cannon by the siege of 1422, using "falcons", which were short but wide cannon. The two sides were evenly matched technologically, and the Turks had to build barricades "in order to receive... the stones of the bombards." Because the Empire at this time was facing economic problems, Pope Pius II promoted the affordable donation of cannon by European monarchs as a means of aid. Any new cannon after the 1422 siege were gifts from European states, and aside from these, no other advances were made to the Byzantine arsenal.

the Dardanelles Gun, a heavy bronze cannon, similar to those at the Siege of Constantinople in 1453

In contrast, when Sultan Mehmet II laid siege to Constantinople in April 1453, he used 68 Hungarian-made cannon, the largest of which was 26 feet (7.9 m) long and weighed 20 tons. This fired a 1,200 pound stone cannonball, and required an operating crew of 200 men. Two such bombards had initially been offered to the Byzantines by the Hungarian artillery expert Urban, which were the pinnacle of gunpowder technology at the time; he boasted that they could reduce "even the walls of Babylon". However, the fact that the Byzantines could not afford it illustrates the financial costs of artillery at the time. These cannon also needed 70 oxen and 10,000 men just to transport them. They were extremely loud, adding to their psychological impact, and Mehmet believed that those who unexpectedly heard it would be struck dumb.

The 55 day bombardment of Constantinople left massive destruction, as recounted by the Greek chronicler Kritovoulos:
And the stone, borne with enormous force and velocity, hit the wall, which it immediately shook and knocked down and was itself broken into many fragments and scattered, hurling the pieces everywhere and killing those who happened to be nearby.

Byzantine counter artillery allowed them to repel any visible Turkish weapons, and the defenders repulsed any attempts to storm any broken points in the walls and hastily repaired any damage. However, the walls could not be adapted for artillery, and towers were not good gun emplacements. There was even worry that the largest Byzantine cannon could cause more damage to their own walls than the Turkish cannon. Gunpowder had also made the formerly devastating Greek fire obsolete, and with the final fall of what had once been the strongest walls in Europe on May 29, "it was the end of an era in more ways than one".

Cannon at the end of the Middle Ages

Toward the end of the Middle Ages, the development of cannon made revolutionary changes to siege warfare throughout Europe, with many castles becoming susceptible to artillery fire. The primary aims in castle wall construction were height and thickness, but these became obsolete because they could be damaged by cannonballs.

The rounded walls of the 14th century Sarzana Castle showed adaption to gunpowder.

Inevitably, many fortifications previously deemed impregnable proved inadequate in the face of gunpowder. The walls and towers of fortifications had to become lower and wider, and by the 1480s, "Italian tracing" had been developed, which used the corner bastion as the basis of fortifications for centuries to come. The introduction of artillery to siege warfare in the Middle Ages made geometry the main element of European military architecture.

In 16th century England, Henry VIII began building Device Forts between 1539 and 1540 as artillery fortresses to counter the threat of invasion from France and Spain. They were built by the state at strategic points for the first powerful cannon batteries, such as Deal Castle, which was perfectly symmetrical, with a low, circular keep at its centre. Over 200 cannon and gun ports were set within the walls, and the fort was essentially a firing platform, with a shape that allowed many lines of fire; its low curved bastions were designed to deflect cannon balls.

To guard against artillery and gunfire, increasing use was made of earthen, brick and stone breastworks and redoubts, such as the geometric fortresses of the 17th century French Marquis de Vauban. Although the obsolescence of castles as fortifications was hastened by the developments of cannon from the 14th century on, many medieval castles still managed to "put up a prolonged resistance" against artillery during the English Civil War of 17th century.

See also
- Early thermal weapons

Footnotes

References
- *Encyclopedia Britannica* (1771). London.
- Bag, A. K. (2005). *Fathullah Shirazi: Cannon, Multi-barrel Gun and Yarghu*. Indian Journal of History of Science.
- Bennet, Matthew; Connolly, Peter (1998). *The Hutchinson Dictionary of Ancient & Medieval Warfare*. contributors John Gillingham and John Lazenby. Taylor & Francis. ISBN 1579581161.
- Bottomley, Frank (1983). *The Castle Explorer's Guide*. Crown Publishers. ISBN 0517421720.
- Bradbury, Jim (1992). *The Medieval Siege*. Rochester, New York: Boydell & Brewer. pp. 390. ISBN 0-85115-312-7. Retrieved 2008-05-26.
- Braun, Wernher Von; Frederick Ira Ordway (1967). *History of Rocketry & Space Travel*. Thomas Y. Crowell Co.. ISBN 0690005881.
- Brodie, Fawn McKay; Brodie, Bernard (1973). *From Crossbow to H-Bomb*. Bloomington: Indiana University Press. ISBN 0-253-20161-6.
- Carman, W.Y.. *A History of Firearms: From Earliest Times to 1914*. New York: Dover Publications. ISBN 0-486-43390-0.
- Chartrand, René (2005-03-20). *French Fortresses in North America 1535–1763: Quebec, Montreal, Louisbourg and New Orleans*. Osprey Publishing. ISBN 9781841767147.
- Gat, Azar (2006). *War in Human Civilization*. New York City: Oxford University Press. pp. 839. ISBN 0-19-926213-6.
- Hoffmeyer, Ada Bruhn de (1972). *Arms and Armour in Spain*. Madrid: Instituto do Estudios sobre Armas Antiguas, Consejo Superior de Investigaciones Científicas, Patronato Menendez y Pelayo. ISBN 0435–029x.
- Gernet, Jacques (1996). *A History of Chinese Civilisation*. Cambridge University Press. ISBN 0-521-49781-7.
- Manucy, Albert (1994-04-01). *Artillery Through the Ages: A Short Illustrated History of Cannon, Emphasizing Types Used in America*. Diane publishing. pp. 97. ISBN 0788107453. Retrieved 2008-05-26.
- Mariana, Juan de. *Historia general de Espana*, 2 volumes, Madrid, 1608, ii, 27; English translation by Captain John Stephens, *The General History of Spain*, 2 parts, London, 1699, p 2 64
- Miller, Douglas; Embleton, Gerry (1979). *The Swiss at War 1300-1500*. Illustrated by Gerry Embleton. Osprey Publishing. pp. 52. ISBN 0-85045-334-8.
- Needham, Joseph (1986). *Science and Civilization in China: Volume 5, Part 7*. Taipei: Caves Books, Ltd.
- Nicolle, David (2000). *Crécy 1346: Triumph of the Longbow*. Osprey Publishing. pp. 102. ISBN 9781855329669.
- Nossov, Konstantin; *Ancient and Medieval Siege Weapons*, UK: Spellmount Ltd, 2006. ISBN 186227343X
- Nossov, Konstantin (2007). *Medieval Russian Fortresses AD 862–1480*. Osprey Publishing. ISBN 9781846030932.
- Partington, J. R., A History of Greek Fire and Gunpowder, reprint by Johns Hopkins University Press, p. 191 (Latin text of Zurita)
- Sadler, John; Walsh, Stephen (2006-05-30). *Flodden 1513: Scotland's Greatest Defeat*. Osprey Publishing. pp. 100. ISBN 9781841769592.
- Turnbull, Stephen; Dennis, Peter (2004-10-22). *The Walls of Constantinople AD 413–1453*. Osprey Publishing. pp. 70. ISBN 1-84176-759-X.
- Watson, R. *Chemical Essays*, vol. I, London, 1787, 1999.
- Wilkinson, Philip (1997-09-09). *Pockets: Castles*. Dorling Kindersley. ISBN 978-0789420473.

External links
- Video Demonstration of the Medieval Siege Society's Medieval style Guns, Including showing ignition of Gun Powder

Source http://en.wikipedia.org/wiki/Gunpowder_artillery_in_the_Middle_Ages

Mons Meg

Sideview

Mons Meg is a medieval supergun now located at Edinburgh Castle, Scotland. There are conflicting theories about its origins, but it appears from the accounts of Philip the Good, Duke of Burgundy that it was made to his order around 1449 and sent as a gift 8 years later to King James II of Scotland, with other artillery supplies.

History

The bombard was manufactured from longitudinal bars of iron, hooped with rings fused into one mass. The Duke's artillery maker Jehan Cambier constructed it, and it was successfully tested at Mons (in the County of Hainaut in Wallonia) in June 1449; however, the Duke did not take delivery of the Mons Meg until 1453. Desiring to "interfere in English affairs", the Duke decided to help the Scots against the English. Mons Meg weighs 15,366 pounds (6,970 kg), is 15 feet (4.6 m) in length, and has a calibre of 20 inches (510 mm). The final cost of the gun was £1,536. 2s.

Burst iron ring which put the cannon out of use

A conflicting theory, based on limited evidence, suggests it was constructed in order to aid James II in the 1452 siege of Threave Castle in the Stewartry of Kirkcudbright, when the Clan MacLellan used it to batter the castle.

The 20-inch (510 mm) calibre cannon accepted balls that weighed about 400 pounds (180 kg), although it could only be fired 8-10 times a day due to the tremendous heat generated by the powder charge required. It has been suggested that Meg was one of the armaments on James IV's carrack, the *Great Michael*, which would make it the ship with the largest calibre gun in history. In early years the gun, like the other royal cannon, was painted with red-lead to keep it from rusting. This cost 30 shillings in June 1539. From the 1540s Meg was retired from active service and was fired only on ceremonial occasions from Edinburgh Castle, from where shot could be found up to two miles distant. When Mons was fired on 3 July 1558, workmen were paid to find and retrieve the shot from Wardie Mure, near the River Forth. The salute marked the solemnization of the marriage of Mary, Queen of Scots to the French Dauphin.

The gun was fired in 1680 to celebrate the arrival of James Duke of Albany and York, later King James II of England and VII of Scotland, when the barrel burst. An English cannoneer had loaded the charge and many Scots believed that the damage was done on purpose out of jealousy, because the English had no cannon as big as this. The incident was also seen as a bad omen for the future King.

The cannon was left outside Foog's Gate at Edinburgh Castle. It was next taken, with other disused ordnance, to the Tower of London in 1754, but was returned to the Castle in 1829, after the intervention of Sir Walter Scott. Following a restoration, it now sits outside St. Margaret's Chapel.

"Mons Meg was a large old-fashioned piece of ordnance, a great favourite with the Scottish common people; she was fabricated at Mons, in Flanders, in the reign of James IV. or V. of Scotland. This gun figures frequently in the public accounts of the time, where we find charges for grease, to grease Meg's mouth withal (to increase, as every schoolboy knows, the loudness of the report), ribands to deck her carriage, and pipes to play before her when she was brought from the Castle to accompany the Scottish army on any distant expedition. After the Union, there was much popular apprehension that the Regalia of Scotland, and the subordinate Palladium, Mons Meg, would be carried to England to complete the odious surrender of national independence. The Regalia, sequestered from the sight of the public, were generally supposed to have been abstracted in this manner. As for Mons Meg, she remained in the Castle of Edinburgh, till, by order of the Board of Ordnance, she was actually removed to Woolwich about 1757. The Regalia, by his Majesty's special command, have been brought forth from their place of concealment in 1818, and exposed to the view of the people, by whom they must be looked upon with deep associations; and, in this very winter of 1828–9, Mons Meg has been restored to the country, where that, which in every other place or situation was a mere mass of rusty iron, becomes once more a curious monument of antiquity" Notes to *Rob Roy*, Sir Walter Scott.

The gun is not called "Mons Meg" in any contemporary references until 1678. In 1489, she first appears in record as "Monss," and in the painter's account of 1539 she is called; "Monce in the castell," the only piece with an individual name. In 1650 she was noted as "Muckle Meg." "Meg" may either be a reference to Margaret of Denmark, Queen of James III of Scotland, or simply an alliteration, while Mons was one of the locations where the cannon was originally tested. McKenzie records that this class of artillery was known as a *murderer* and Mons Meg was certainly described as such.

Besides the Mons Meg, a number of 15th-century European superguns are known to have been employed primarily in siege warfare, including the wrought-iron pieces Pumhart von Steyr and Dulle Griet as well as the cast-bronze Faule Mette, Faule Grete and Grose Bochse.

During the Hogmanay celebrations of 2009/2010 the District Gunner Sgt Jamie Shannon (also known as "Shannon the Cannon") fired Mons Meg from Edinburgh Castle. A cannonball was placed inside the weapon for visual effect, while the powder was ignited by use of a car battery.

Evolution of the carriage

Mons Meg at Edinburgh Castle in the 1680s, showing details of the carriage construction

For a while in its early days the Mons sat on a plain box without any wheels. Evidently, when Mons Meg was removed from Edinburgh Castle in 1754, her carriage had long since rotted away. A contemporary account describes her as lying "on the ground" near the innermost gate to the castle. Presumably the Ordnance Board fabricated a new carriage after her arrival at the Tower.

In 1835, after the return of Mons Meg to Edinburgh Castle, the London-made carriage rotted away too and fabrication of a cast-iron replacement was undertaken.

As we see Mons Meg today, it is mounted on a reproduction of the carriage depicted in a stone carving of ca. 1500 on a wall of Edinburgh Castle.

Source http://en.wikipedia.org/wiki/Mons_Meg

Ribauldequin

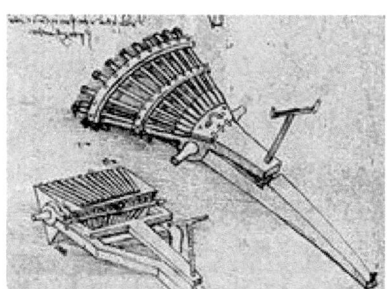

A drawing of a ribauldequin, as designed by Leonardo Da Vinci.

A **Ribauldequin**, also known as a **rabauld**, **ribault**, **ribaudkin**, or **organ gun**, was a late medieval volley gun with many small-caliber iron barrels set up parallel on a platform, in use during the 14th and 15th centuries. When the gun was fired in a volley, it created a shower of iron shot. They were employed, specifically, during the early fifteenth century, and continued serving, mostly, as an anti-personnel gun.

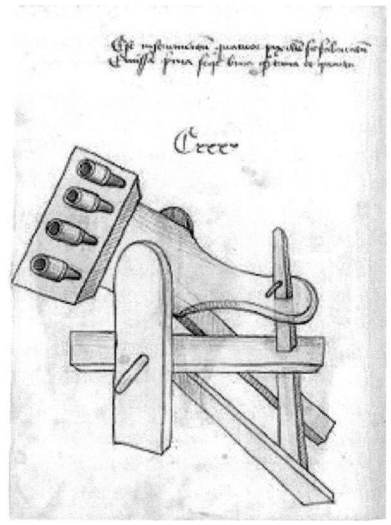

Organ gun in the Bellifortis treatise (ca. 1405)

As an early type of multiple barrel firearm, the *ribauldequin* is sometimes considered the predecessor of the 19th century mitrailleuse.

The first known ribauldequin was used by the army of Edward III of England in 1339 in France during the Hundred Years War. Edward's ribauldequins had twelve barrels which fired salvoes of twelve balls. Nine-barreled ribaults were used by Milan and other participants in the Italian Wars. Ribauldequins were also used in the Wars of the Roses. During the Second Battle of St Albans, Burgundian soldiers under Yorkist control utilized the weapon against the Lancastrian Army led by Queen Margaret of Anjou. In Eastern Europe, a heavier version of the organ gun was used by Stephen the Great of Moldavia as late as 1475, as attested to by Polish chronicler Bieski.

Source http://en.wikipedia.org/wiki/Ribauldequin

Trebuchet

Trebuchets at Château de Castelnaud

A **trebuchet** (/ˈtrɛbəʃɛt/ *treb-ə-shet* or /ˌtrɛbjuˈʃɛt/ *treb-ew-shet*; French: *trébuchet*) is a siege engine that was employed in the Middle Ages. It is sometimes called a "counterweight trebuchet" or "counterpoise trebuchet" in order to distinguish it from an earlier weapon that has come to be called the "traction trebuchet", the original version

Counterweight trebuchet constructed on the design of the "Warwolf"

with pulling men instead of a counterweight. Man-powered trebuchets appeared in the Greek world and China in about the 4th century BC.

The counterweight trebuchet appeared in both Christian and Muslim

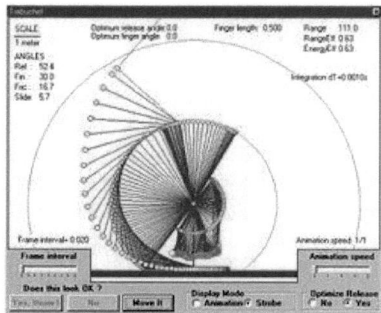

A strobe picture of a simulated trebuchet in action

lands around the Mediterranean in the twelfth century. It could fling projectiles of up to three hundred and fifty pounds (140 kg) at high speeds into enemy fortifications.

The trebuchet did not become obsolete until the 15th century, well after the

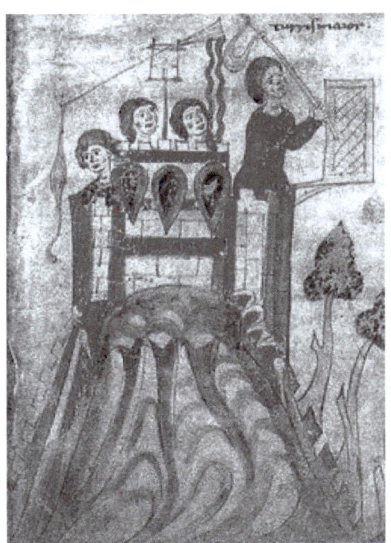

Medieval traction trebuchet next to a staff slinger

introduction of gunpowder, which appeared in Europe in second half of 13th century.

A trebuchet is a type of catapult that works by using the energy of a raised counterweight to throw the projectile. Initially, the sling, which has a pouch containing the projectile, is placed in a trough below the axle, which supports the beam. Upon releasing the trigger, the sling and the beam swing around toward the vertical position, where one end of the sling releases, opening the pouch and propelling the projectile towards the target. The efficiency of the transfer of the stored energy of the counterweight to the projectile can be quite high, even without, for example, restraining the path of the counterweight.

Modern-day enthusiasts have varied the original design, especially to control the path of the counterweight.

Trebuchets versus torsion

The trebuchet is often confused with the earlier torsion siege engines. The main difference is that a torsion siege engine (examples of which include the onager and ballista) uses a twisted rope or twine to provide power, whereas a trebuchet uses a counterweight, usually much closer to the fulcrum than the payload for mechanical advantage, though this is not necessary. A trebuchet also has a sling holding the projectile (although the Roman onager often had a sling as well), and a means for releasing it at the right moment for maximum range.

History

Traction trebuchet

11th century chronicle depicting a Byzantine siege.

The trebuchet derives from the ancient sling. A variation of the sling, called staff sling (Latin: *fustibalus*), contained a short piece of wood to extend the arm and provide greater leverage. This evolved into the traction trebuchet in which a number of people pull on ropes attached to the short arm of a lever that has a sling on the long arm. This type of trebuchet is smaller and has a shorter range, but is a more portable machine and has a faster rate of fire than larger, counterweight-powered types. The smallest traction trebuchets could be powered by the weight and pulling strength of one person using a single rope, but most were designed and sized for between 15 and 45 men, generally two per rope. These teams would sometimes be local citizens helping in the siege or in the defense of their town. Traction trebuchets had a range of 100 to 200 feet (30 to 61 m) when casting weights up to 250 pounds (110 kg). It is believed that the first traction trebuchets were used by the Mohists in China as early as in the 5th century BC descriptions of which can be found in the *Mojing* (compiled in the 4th century BC). The Chinese named the later counterweight trebuchet Huihui Pao (Muslim Weapons, "huihui" means Muslim) or Xiangyang Pao (襄陽砲), where Pao means bombard.

The traction trebuchet next appeared in Byzantium. The *Strategikon* of Emperor Maurice, composed in the late 6th century, calls for "ballistae revolving in both directions," (Βαλλίστρας εκατηρωθεν στρεφόμενας), probably traction trebuchets (Dennis 1998, p. 99). The *Miracles of St. Demetrius*, composed by John I, archbishop of Thessalonike, clearly describe traction trebuchets in the Avaro-Slav artillery: "Hanging from the back sides of these pieces of timber were slings and from the front strong ropes, by which, pulling down and releasing the sling, they propel the stones up high and with a loud noise." (John I 597 1:154, ed. Lemerle 1979)

They were also used with great effect by the Islamic armies during the Muslim conquests. A surviving Arab technical treatise on these machines is Kitab Aniq fi al-Manajaniq (كتاب أنيق في المنجنيق, *An Elegant Book on Trebuchets*), written in 1462 by Yusuf ibn Urunbugha al-Zaradkash. It provides detailed construction and operating information.

There is some doubt as to the exact period in which traction trebuchets, or knowledge of them, reached Scandinavia. The Vikings may have known of them at a very early stage, as the monk Abbo de St. Germain reports on the siege of Paris in his epic *De bello Parisiaco* dated about 890 that engines of war were used. Another source mentions that Nordic people or "the Norsemen" used engines of war at the siege of Angers as early as 873.

Hand-trebuchet

The hand-trebuchet (Greek: cheiromangana) was a staff sling mounted on a pole using a lever mechanism to propel projectiles. Basically a portable trebuchet which could be operated by a single man, it was used by emperor Nikephoros II Phokas around 965 to disrupt enemy formations in the open field. It was also mentioned in the Taktika of general Nikephoros Ouranos (ca. 1000), and listed in the *Anonymus De obsidione toleranda* as a form of artillery

Counterweight trebuchet

Counterweight trebuchet at Château des Baux, France

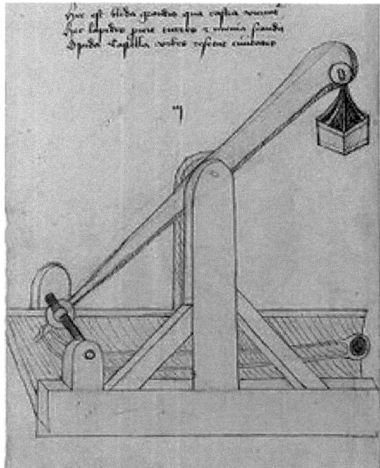

Counterweight trebuchet by the German engineer Konrad Kyeser (ca. 1405)

Side view of counterweight trebuchet

19th century French three-quarter drawing of a medieval counterweight trebuchet

The earliest written record of the counterweight trebuchet, much more powerful than the traction version, appears in the work of the 12th century Byzantine historian Niketas Choniates. Niketas describes a trebuchet used by Andronikos I Komnenos, future Byzantine emperor, at the siege of Zevgminon in 1165 which was equipped with a windlass, an apparatus which was required neither for traction nor hybrid trebuchets to launch missiles. Chevedden dates the invention of the new artillery type back to the Siege of Nicaea in 1097 when the Byzantine emperor Alexios I Komnenos, an ally of the besieging crusaders, was reported to have invented new pieces of heavy artillery which deviated from the conventional design and made a deep impression on everyone.

The dramatic increase in military performance is for the first time reflected in historical records on the occasion of the second siege of Tyre in 1124, when the crusaders reportedly made use of "great trebuchets". By the 1120–30s, the counterweight trebuchet had diffused not only to the crusaders states, but probably also westwards to the Normans of Sicily and eastwards to the Great Seljuqs. The military use of the new gravity-powered artillery culminated in the 12th century during the Siege of Acre (1189–91) which saw the kings Richard I of England and Philip II of France wrestle for control of the city with Saladin's forces.

The only pictorial evidence of a counterweight trebuchet in the 12th century comes from an Islamic scholar, Mardi bin Ali al-Tarsusi, who wrote a military manual for Saladin circa 1187 based on information collected from an Armenian weapon expert in Muslim service. He describes a hybrid trebuchet that he said had the same hurling power as a traction machine pulled by fifty men due to "the constant force [of gravity], whereas men differ in their pulling force." (Showing his mechanical proficiency, Tarsusi designed his trebuchet so that as it was fired it cocked a supplementary crossbow, probably to protect the engineers from attack.) He allegedly wrote "Trebuchets are machines invented by unbelieving devils." (Al-Tarsusi, Bodleian MS 264). This suggests that by the time of Saladin, Muslims were acquainted with counterweight engines, but did not believe that they had invented these machines.

During the Crusades, Philip II of France named two of the trebuchets he used in the Siege of Acre in 1191 "God's Stone-Thrower" and "Bad Neighbor." During a siege of Stirling Castle in 1304, Edward Longshanks ordered his engineers to make a giant trebuchet for the English army, named "Warwolf". Range and size of the weapons varied. In 1421 the future Charles VII of France commissioned a trebuchet (*coyllar*) that could shoot a stone of 800 kg, while in 1188 at Ashyun, rocks up to 1,500 kg were used. Average weight of the projectiles was probably around 50–100 kg, with a range of ca. 300 meters. Rate of fire could be noteworthy: at the siege of Lisbon (1147), two engines were capable of launching a stone every 15 seconds. Also human corpses could be used in special occasion: in 1422 Prince Korybut, for example, in the siege of Karlštejn Castle shot men and manure within the enemy walls, apparently managing to spread infection among the defenders. The largest trebuchets needed exceptional quantities of timber: at the Siege of Damietta, in 1249, Louis IX of France was able to build a stockade for the whole Crusade camp with the wood from 24 captured Egyptian trebuchets.

Counterweight trebuchets do not appear with certainty in Chinese historical records until about 1268, when the Mongols laid siege to Fancheng and Xiangyang. At the Siege of Fancheng and Xiangyang, the Mongol army, unable to capture the cities despite besieging the Song defenders for years, brought in two Persian engineers who built hinged counterweight trebuchets and soon reduced the cities to rubble, forcing the surrender of the garrison. These engines were called by the Chinese historians the Huihui Pao (回回砲)("huihui" means Muslim) or Xiangyang Pao (襄陽砲), because they were first encountered in that battle. Recent research by Paul E. Chevedden indicates that the *hui-hui pao* was actually a European design, a double-counterweight engine that had been introduced to the Levant by Holy Roman Emperor Frederick II (1210–1250) only shortly before. The Muslim historian Rashid-al-Din Hamadani (1247?–1318) refers in his universal history to the Mongol trebuchets used at the Song cities as "Frankish" or "European trebuchets" ("manjaniq ifranji" or "manjaniq firanji"):

Before that there had not been any large Frankish catapult in Cathay [i.e. China], but Talib, a catapult-maker from this land, had gone to Baalbek and Damascus, and his sons Abubakr, Ibrahim, and Muhammad, and his employees made seven large catapults and set out to conquer the city [Sayan Fu or Hsiang-yang fu = modern Xiangfan].

With the introduction of gunpowder, the trebuchet lost its place as the siege engine of choice to the cannon. Trebuchets were used both at the siege of Burgos (1475–1476) and siege of Rhodes (1480). One of the last recorded military uses was by Hernán Cortés, at the 1521 siege of the Aztec capital Tenochtitlán. Accounts of the attack note that its use was motivated by the limited supply of gunpowder. The attempt was reportedly unsuccessful: the first projectile landed on the trebuchet itself, destroying it.

In 1779, British forces defending Gibraltar, finding that their cannons were unable to fire far enough for some purposes, constructed a trebuchet. It is unknown how successful this was: the Spanish attackers were eventually defeated, but this was largely due to a sortie.

Modern recreational use

Trebuchets are popular in modern times in a number of contexts. In particular, traditional models are constructed by historical re-enactment and living history enthusiasts, and others use the trebuchet as an engineering challenge, or for recreational purposes. Traction Trebuchets can be hired for functions, festivals, Stag do and other outdoor events.

Trebuchets are used to throw pumpkins at the annual pumpkin chunking contest held in Sussex County, Delaware. The record-holder in that contest for trebuchets is the Yankee Siege, which at the 2009 Championship tossed a pumpkin 2,034 feet (620 m). The 51-foot-tall (16 m), 55,000-pound (25,000 kg) trebuchet fires 8–10-pound (3.6–4.5 kg) pumpkins.

The largest currently-functioning trebuchet in the world is the 22-tonne machine at Warwick Castle, England. It stands 18 metres tall (59 ft) and throws missiles typically 80lbs up to 300 metres.

Modern engineering thought and materials have come up with several non-traditional designs, in particular, several with "floating arms" to increase efficiency.

Floating-arm trebuchet

Trebuchet in Denmark

A floating-arm trebuchet is an efficient modern variant. Rather than having an axle fixed to the frame, it is mounted on wheels that roll on a track parallel to the ground, and the counterweight is constrained to fall in a direct path downwards upon the release. This increases the proportion of energy transferred to the projectile. This is more sophisticated than the medieval weapon, but previous designs accomplished a similar effect by placing the whole trebuchet on wheels.

Source http://en.wikipedia.org/wiki/Trebuchet